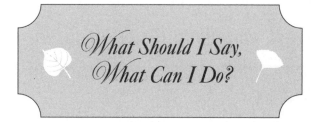

What Should I Say,
What Can I Do?

What Should I Say, What Can I Do?

HOW TO
REACH OUT TO
THOSE YOU LOVE

Rebecca Bram Feldbaum

Pocket Books

New York   London   Toronto   Sydney

Pocket Books
A Division of Simon & Schuster, Inc.
1230 Avenue of the Americas
New York, NY 10020

First Pocket Books hardcover edition August 2008

POCKET and colophon are registered trademarks of Simon & Schuster, Inc.

For information about special discounts for bulk purchases, please contact Simon & Schuster Special Sales at 1-800-456-6798 or business@simonandschuster.com.

Designed by Jill Weber

Manufactured in the United States of America

10 9 8 7 6 5 4 3 2 1

Library of Congress Cataloging-in-Publication Data

Feldbaum, Rebecca Bram.
   What should I say, what can I do?: how to reach out to those you love /
Rebecca Bram Feldbaum.

ISBN-13: 978-1-4165-5717-3
ISBN-10:   1-4165-5717-2

  1. Grief. 2. Bereavement—Psychological aspects. I. Title.
   BF575.G7F465 2008
   155.9'37—dc22

                                           2007048959

THIS BOOK IS DEDICATED
TO THE MEMORY OF
DINA BLAUSTEIN,

A person who truly epitomized
what it means to help a friend in need

Acknowledgments

For making this book possible, I extend my heartfelt thanks to . . .

GOD, for all He has done for me and my children. I hope that He continues to bless my family with all of His bountiful goodness.

My Mother, Lillian Tron Bram, for all of your love and encouragement through the years. All of my success stems from you. My father, Abraham Bram, for watching over my family "from above."

My children, Raizel, Chaya Gittel, Moshe, and Michoel Simcha, who were so understanding of all the time I spent writing this book. No words can possibly describe the incredible joy I get from each one of you every single day. And, to my brand-new son-in-law, Doniel Simcha Keilson, Raizel's husband, for adding such "simcha" (happiness) into our family.

My sister-in-law and brother, Hadar and Harris Bram, for all that you have done and continue to do for me and your nieces and nephews.

My "Baltimore Buddies," Pepi Cohen, Dina Cotton, Chava Drebin, Pam Kanter, Connie Lazar, and Rebekka Ottensoser, and my "Out-of-Town Buddies," Gloria Feldman, Rona Holzer, and Mary Zinstein, for your constant support and your encouragement to keep on writing!

My office coworkers, Brina Insel and Mimi Biegacz, who covered for me for months so I could take off every Wednesday ("writing Wednesday") and write this book. *And to my wonderful boss, Judy Gross,* who has been behind me one hundred percent since the inception of this book.

To my literary agent at Writer's House, Al Zuckerman, for truly believing in me and doing your utmost to get this book published. *And to Daniel Lazar,* who showed my first book to Al and set all of this in motion.

To the editorial director of Pocket Books, Maggie Crawford, who saw my original manuscript and was able to envision a Pocket Books version. I hope that I fulfilled all of your expectations of what this book should offer the public.

And last but by no means least, my terrific editor at Pocket Books, Micki Nuding. Your insightful suggestions and encouraging words helped keep me focused and enthusiastic while I was writing this book.

Contents

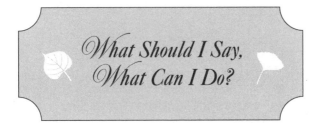

What Should I Say,
What Can I Do?

INTRODUCTION

Certain situations in our lives are permanently cemented in our memories. They have such a profound effect on us that we can't seem to shake the feelings that surface with those memories. These are called life-changing experiences because that is exactly what they are—experiences that change our lives forever.

My life-changing experience divided my life into two parts. The first part of my life consists of my childhood, teenage years, college experiences, first job, traveling, marriage, and becoming a mother.

The second half of my life began when my husband of nine years, Robert (Bobby) Feldbaum, died, leaving me a young widow. I was thirty-seven years old and the mother of four young children, the oldest only seven. At that moment my entire world changed into something completely different.

When a person suffers such a devastating loss, he can't come out of his abyss of grief without help from his friends and family. These wonderful people, who care about us so much and who would do anything for us, are such an important part of our lives. Their love and support are what help keep our heads above water so we don't drown in our profound sorrow.

This book is a compilation of the ways family and friends reached out to me and my children when my husband was sick and after he died. Many of the suggestions offered in this book are based on things that personally happened to us. Other advice I either read about or heard directly from others who suffered a loss. Every widow/er I spoke to was in complete agreement with me that the love and support offered by our friends and family members is truly priceless.

Sometimes I wonder at what point I really appreciated all of the help and caring showered on me by friends and family members.

- Was it when my neighbors sent over their teenage daughters to help take care of my children so I could exclusively attend to the needs of my very sick husband?

- Was it when a friend came to the hospital when Bobby was undergoing a medical procedure, so I wouldn't have to sit in the waiting room by myself?

- Was it when a friend held me close immediately after Bobby died, and said, "You were a wonderful wife. You did everything you could for him. Now we will be here for you and your children"?

- Was it when my family members and friends sent delicious home-cooked and takeout dinners to my home for a full month after Bobby died?

- Was it when I had a horrible migraine headache from all of the new-widow pressures and a friend rubbed my back for hours as I sobbed into my pillow?

- Was it when I was having a hard time financially and people came to my aid?

- Was it at my oldest child's high school graduation, where so many of my friends surprised me by showing up?

- Was it at the first wedding I attended as a widow, when a friend came over to me and said, "I am so glad that you came, Becca. It's marvelous to see you."

- Was it when I received a beautiful piece of jewelry from my close friends on the occasion of a particularly meaningful event I was celebrating?

- Was it when a friend's husband took my young sons to a store to help "fit them" for the right baseball gloves and then showed them how to throw a curve ball?

Every one of the thoughtful acts directed toward me and my children was so greatly appreciated; each one made such a difference in my life and the lives of my children. Those kindnesses helped keep me happy, focused, and sane.

This book will explain what you can do for, and what you should say to, a person going through the illness and death of a loved one. After you finish reading it, you will definitely have some ideas of your own about how to help someone you love and care about. So, run with those ideas! And if they work out well, don't forget to tell everyone. We can all benefit from learning new ways to help those in need.

Hospital Visits and Gifts

GUIDELINES FOR VISITORS

*F*ollowing are ways people can make a hospital visit that is appreciated by the patient and her family. Many of these guidelines also apply to visiting a sick patient at home.

❧ *Call ahead of time to see if the patient wants visitors.*

If the patient is not up to visitors, there are innumerable other ways to help out his family. (Read the chapter "Helping the Caregiver" for suggestions.) Or the family may want you to come to the hospital to stay with the patient so that they can go home for a few hours. Ask what they need help with the most—and be prepared for their answer.

❧ *Never visit a patient in the hospital if you are not feeling well.*

Even a "slight" cold can have serious repercussions for patients, especially those undergoing treatments and the elderly. Even if cold or flu symptoms have not manifested themselves, don't take the chance of infecting hospitalized patients. People who are sick are weak and much more susceptible to catching something contagious, which can have an adverse effect on their recovery.

🌸 *Don't make a hospital visit with a large group of people.*

Three is the maximum number of visitors who should congregate in a hospital room at one time. The patient won't be able to concentrate on the conversation with too many people surrounding him. Also, it's very disturbing to a patient when there is too much noise and activity in his room.

🌸 *Children shouldn't visit patients in the hospital.*

An exception to this rule is when a parent, sibling, or grandparent in the hospital especially requests to see them. Check with your pediatrician first about bringing newborns to the hospital. If the children or grandchildren are not allowed to visit the patient, they can decorate cards, make tape recordings, write letters, or draw colorful signs for her.

◆ *Bring food to the patient that you are certain she is allowed to eat.*

Many patients are not allowed to eat certain foods because they're not good for them, such as highly salted foods for heart patients. Always check with family members or at the nurses' station before offering a patient outside food.

◆ *Come to the hospital as "odorless" as possible.*

Patients in the hospital who are undergoing treatments are very sensitive to odors. When you visit do not wear perfume, cologne, or any type of soap, hand or body lotion, or deodorant that has a lingering aroma. These can make your visit unbearable to some- one who is fighting nausea.

🌿 *Always knock on the patient's door before entering the room.*

If you don't hear a "come in" response, check at the nurses' station before entering. The patient may be undergoing a minor medical procedure, may not be fully clothed, may be in the bathroom, or may be sleeping. Remember, patients have the right to maintain some privacy within a hospital setting.

🌿 *If the patient is sleeping, don't disturb her.*

Unless the patient gave you explicit instructions to wake her when you arrived, let her sleep. Leave a note for her at the nurses' station or in her room. The patient needs her rest, and a note will be just as appreciated as a "real visit."

Turn off your cell phone before entering the room.

You need to give the patient your undivided attention. He wants to enjoy interacting with you, which can't be done if you're constantly talking on your cell phone. You can, however, ask the patient if he would like you to answer his ringing hospital phone or place a call for him.

Be prepared for how the patient will look.

If you aren't able to visit the patient without holding back your emotions, you shouldn't visit her. The last thing she needs to see is you gasping, staring, or crying in reaction to her appearance. This only depresses the patient if she feels she looks horribly different (which she might). Enter her room with a smile on your face and make direct eye contact.

🌿 *Be prepared for how the patient will behave.*

The patient may be undergoing a temporary personality change. He may exhibit signs of a short attention span, be exceptionally quiet, or be quite angry and volatile. This could be a reaction to the medications he's taking or an emotional response to his medical situation. If the patient says anything that shocks you, refrain from commenting and instead show your support by being a listening, caring friend.

🌿 *Do not sit or place your purse or coat on the patient's bed.*

The patient's surroundings need to be kept as sterile as possible. You never know what you may have brought in from the outside world that contains germs. Remember, you are there to make the patient feel more comfortable, not the other way around!

Don't have any physical contact with the patient unless he makes the first gesture.

Many patients are sore from the various treatments they are receiving, or achy from being in bed so long. Even a kiss, hug, or handshake could be painful to him. Your safest bet is to blow the patient a kiss. Let him make the first move toward you before you reach out to him. If he wants his hand held or his back massaged, do it very lightly and gently.

Don't read the patient's medical chart.

No matter how well-meaning your intentions, this is a complete invasion of the patient's privacy. If you are not his doctor or a member of the hospital staff, don't casually glance over any personal medical papers.

🌸 *Depending on how the patient is feeling, limit your visit to fifteen to thirty minutes.*

If the patient is lonely or scared or just plain bored and sincerely wants you to stay longer, that's fine, of course. But don't think that you have to entertain her; your quiet presence may be all she needs.

🌸 *Don't ask the patient about her condition.*

It is the patient's prerogative to discuss or not discuss her illness. If she completely avoids speaking about her medical condition, follow her lead. But if she does make reference to it, let her guide the conversation, and be careful not to pry and put her in an uncomfortable position. Don't bring up stories of family members who were stricken with the same disease and describe their unfortunate outcomes. Also, she doesn't want to hear about all of your latest medical issues.

🌷 *Be considerate of the patient's roommates.*

Don't make too much noise that would disturb the roommates. Pull the curtain between the beds to maximize privacy. If you're getting something for the patient (for example, from the hospital cafeteria), it's polite to ask his roommate if he'd like something also.

🌷 *Have normal conversations with the patient.*

Don't talk in a condescending way to the patient. For various reasons—her medical condition or the medicines she's taking—she may not be able to concentrate as well as she used to, but that doesn't mean she should be spoken down to. (This advice especially holds true for elderly patients.)

● *Conversations about the patient should be held in the hallway.*

Never assume that just because she's critically ill a patient doesn't understand what you're saying about her condition. Also don't assume she's "fully asleep" when her eyes are closed. And never underestimate what hospitalized children or teenagers can understand.

● *When the patient's doctor enters the room, excuse yourself and walk out of earshot.*

Even if the doctor tells you to stay, you should leave the room. Only close friends or family members who are absolutely certain the patient wants them in the room should stay. This may be the only time during the day that the patient will be able to discuss personal matters with her physician, and she should be given the privacy to do so.

GIFT GIVING

Whether visiting an ill person in the hospital or at home, people do not like to arrive empty-handed. Some points to keep in mind:

1. The best presents to bring to the hospital are throw-away gifts that can be disposed of, or presents that are light and small to pack.

2. It is completely acceptable to send a present to the person's home instead of taking it to the hospital.

3. Do not expect a thank-you note or phone call from the patient or her family. You can call to make sure the present did arrive.

4. When you bring a present to a patient at home, try to bring something for the caregiver and/or children, too, like a home-cooked meal, a batch of cupcakes, a board game, etc.

5. Don't forget to bring a token of appreciation for the hard-working nursing staff—a bagel-and-cream-cheese platter for breakfast, doughnuts or homemade cookies for snacks, or a vegetable/fruit platter for lunch or dinner. A letter to the hospital administrator about the exceptional care your loved one received is a very nice gesture, too.

Gift Ideas

Here are some suggestions for presents that hospital patients really like receiving; many of the items make wonderful gifts to give to the patient at home, too.

- *A favorite newspaper or magazine.*

   The hospital may not sell it and the patient will really enjoy reading his favorite periodical. It makes a patient feel good when he can keep up with the most current information on topics he's particularly interested in.

- *A new book by the patient's favorite author.*

   Depending on the dexterity and strength of the patient's hands, the book should be bought in either hardcover or paperback. You can also purchase a stand that will hold the book up for the patient. Don't forget to include a cute bookmark.

🌸 *A new robe or pajamas.*

In many hospitals, the patient is allowed to wear his own robe and pajamas. Pick out a set in his favorite color or, for laughs, one with a cartoon pattern. Ask the family members what kind of material the patient prefers wearing. If he is recovering from surgery, he may want to wear only 100 percent cotton, until his stitches heal.

🌸 *A bouquet of flowers.*

Flowers definitely brighten up a hospital room with their cheeriness and color. Ask the florist for ideas if you don't want to send a large bouquet: you could send flowers in a decorative mug or a small plant, for example. If the patient is in an ICU, check with the nurses first, because some ICUs may not allow flowers/plants that will attract insects around the patient.

◆ *A new CD from the patient's favorite recording artist.*

This is a great gift, as music can be very soothing to patients—especially the music they enjoy listening to. If the patient has an iPod, borrow it for a few hours and download the CD onto it for him.

◆ *The activity/game the patient enjoys doing.*

A crossword puzzle book, a new needlepoint to embroider, a Sudoku book, a new game for his Game Boy, a deck of cards, or even a Rubik's Cube is a nice gift to bring a patient. The present should be able to be done/played by one person. This will keep his mind occupied so he can forget about his medical situation for a little while.

● *The patient's favorite food.*

If she has an appetite, the aroma of her favorite meal or treat wafting through the doorway is a wonderful comfort to a patient. But be sure to check with family members or her nurse before giving outside food to a patient.

● *A calendar.*

It's hard to keep track of time in a hospital, when days and nights seem to blend together. A nice gift is a theme calendar with pictures the patient will enjoy, such as country settings, race cars, animals, or photos of friends, coworkers, or children/grandchildren, in serious or funny poses. Be sure to choose a calendar size that will fit on wall space near the patient's bed. An illuminated watch or clock is also an excellent present as the patient may not be able to read the clock on the wall.

A box of stationery, a new pen, return address labels (if possible), and postage stamps.

Have all these materials ready for patients who feel well enough to write a note to friends and family members. Lined stationery is a good choice for patients whose hands may be shaky.

Toiletry items.

A new brush or comb, small mirror on a stand, shaving case, toothbrush and toothpaste holder, soft makeup case, or a new manicure kit. Patients feel so much better when they can freshen up. Be sure to bring the patient a particular product or brand you know she likes using.

Helping the Caregiver

*H*aving a sick family member takes a toll on everyone in the house. While the ill person becomes the focus of everyone's attention, the main caregiver should not be forgotten, either. Trying to preserve a normal home environment, maintain a job, and take care of the ill person is exhausting, and they need help to maintain their physical and emotional well-being.

WHAT YOU CAN DO TO HELP

There are many ways friends and family members can help out someone taking care of an ill loved one.

Help Them with Their Home

Due to normal wear and tear, things may need to be fixed or replaced. Either help the caregiver fix what's broken or guide her toward someone who can do so. This also applies to the maintenance of her car.

Help Them Maintain Their Yard

Mow their lawn and trim their bushes; remind them to get their gutters cleaned after the fall season or arrange for this to be done; shovel their sidewalk and driveway after a big snowstorm and help them dig their car out of the snow. If you have a green thumb, offer to tend their flower or vegetable garden. These suggestions are especially helpful for an elderly person.

Run Errands

Ask the family what errands they need taken care of. They'll often have a long list of things that have to get done, such as picking up clothes from the cleaners, making a bank deposit, filling up the car with gas, picking up items from the grocery store, buying stamps or mailing letters at the post office, or picking up prescriptions from the pharmacy.

Organize Car Rides

For families with children not old enough to drive, offering rides is a tremendous help. Children need to get back and forth to school and to any after-school activities. Many times it's just not possible for the caregiver to leave the hospital, especially when the patient has a procedure scheduled or if the caregiver is waiting to speak with the patient's doctor.

Take Care of Pets

Offer to feed the family pet and, if necessary, take him for daily walks. If the family is going through a crisis, offer to keep the pet at your house for a few days/weeks until the situation calms down.

Include the Family in Holiday Plans

A family with a critically ill member wants to have a normal holiday celebration just like everyone else, but that could be an impossible undertaking. The main caregiver may not have time for holiday preparations. That's why it's so important to include family members in your celebration. If they prefer a quiet celebration in their own home, help them arrange this.

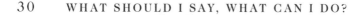

Watch After Youngsters or the Elderly

There are times when the main caregiver needs to get to the hospital but is unable to leave her young children or elderly relatives by themselves. Before you go to the hospital for a visit, call and offer to stay with the children or elderly person instead, giving the caregiver the time to go to the hospital.

Send Over Teenagers to Help

Teenagers can be an absolute lifesaver to the main care-giver. They can give the younger children baths, get them into their pajamas, read to them, and put them to bed; take the children to the library to check out books for school projects and help them write or design those projects; help the children shop for clothes or school supplies; drop them off and pick them up from after-school activities or private lessons; and tutor them in subjects they need a little help with.

Before the Funeral

*W*hen someone dies, the bereaved family needs to be surrounded in a warm, loving cocoon with their closest friends and family members. No matter how prepared a family is for this tragedy, the home of the deceased is usually in a state of turmoil. There are many immediate decisions to be made about which funeral home to contact, where the main service should take place, obtaining a burial plot, the eulogies, and notifying friends and relatives. At this time, designated people can be enormously helpful in the following tasks:

- Take charge of the telephone calls in the house: write down any important messages that need to be relayed to the mourners and make phone calls for them; contact people about when and where the funeral will take place; and find babysitters for the children of the mourners and, if needed, their out-of-town company so that they will be able to attend the funeral.

- Coordinate transportation pickups and overnight accommodations for out-of-towners who've come to attend the funeral.

- Take charge of dealing with the food that is usually sent over as soon as people hear about a death: fruit baskets from coworkers, casseroles from neighbors, vegetable/cheese/ deli platters from friends/relatives.

- Help family members get ready for the funeral, assisting the overly distraught in picking out clothes for them or their children, putting outfits together, and dressing the younger children.

DURING THE FUNERAL

Funerals are hard to attend because no one is untouched by death. As we mourn the passing of someone we will never see again, it is also a sobering reminder of our own mortality. On another level, it means a great deal to the grieving family when they see an outpouring of support from family and friends at the funeral. It truly does help to ease the profound sorrow they are feeling at this time.

Guidelines for Funeral Attendance

🌿 *Never make anyone feel guilty about not attending a funeral.*

Whether a person has a valid reason for attending or skipping a funeral should not be anyone else's concern. People often have very personal reasons for not being able to attend, and their privacy should be respected. They will have opportunities in the weeks following the funeral to show care and concern for the mourners.

🌿 *Dress appropriately.*

This doesn't mean you should wear only dark colors, but flamboyant outfits are not tasteful at this time. Everyone is in a somber mood, and flashy, outlandish clothes don't befit the occasion.

◆ *Ask for guidance regarding the funeral practices of an unfamiliar religion.*

The majority of people don't want to stand out from the crowd or do anything that would be considered inappropriate. Speak to someone before the service to find out how the service is conducted, where you should sit, and how you should dress and behave.

◆ *Sign the guestbook.*

At the entrance to many funeral homes, a sign-in register is made available so the mourners will know who attended the funeral. You can just sign your name; no added messages are necessary. At the funeral, family members are in such a state of grief that they won't be able to remember much. It is a true comfort for them to be able to read the register later and see who attended the funeral.

🌸 *Turn off your cell phone.*

The family won't appreciate a cell phone ringing when the deceased is being eulogized. If you're expecting an important call you can't miss (for example, if you're a doctor), then put your ringer on vibrate and sit in one of the back rows.

🌸 *Say the right thing.*

"I am so sorry for your loss" is an appropriate phrase to use when speaking with the bereaved. It is a polite way to emotionally connect with them at their time of immense heartache and it expresses your own anguish and sense of sorrow at the death of their loved one. Don't try to strike up a lengthy conversation at this time; they need to weep and mourn—so put your arm around them instead.

◆ *Don't discuss the cause of death.*

Family members might not want to discuss how their loved one died, especially if he was murdered, it was an accidental death, he committed suicide, or if the death was drug-related or a communicable disease, etc. They may also want the details of the death kept quiet for the children's sake. Focus on comforting the family and not on the cause of death.

◆ *Do not bring babies or very young children.*

If the children are closely related to the deceased (for example, the deceased is their parent, grandparent, or sibling) their attendance should be discussed ahead of time. As a general rule, funerals are not an appropriate place for babies. There are always extenuating circumstances, such as one of the mourners exclusively nursing her child. Babies should be watched where they will not disturb the service.

🌸 *Videotape or audiotape the funeral.*

Many funeral homes provide this service. The family will be so distraught at the funeral that most likely they won't be able to concentrate fully on the eulogies. If the funeral home where the service is taking place does not offer to do this for the family, record the kind words said about their loved one and make copies for the immediate family members. As a nice gesture, offer to be with them when they hear the tape for the first time.

🌸 *Classmates should come to the funeral of a friend who has lost a parent or sibling.*

The child/teenager feels a great deal of solace when he sees his friends at the funeral of a loved one. Knowing that he has the support of his peers is a tremendous comfort to him. If this is the first time the child or teenager has attended a funeral, he should be told ahead of time about what will occur. Also, an adult should accompany him throughout the service.

Guidelines for Eulogies

People giving the eulogies should keep in mind the following:

🍃 *Very emotional, dramatic speeches can be frightening to children.*

For a child who has lost a parent, this is truly the worst day of his life. He is scared enough about his loss, what is going on in his home, and the solemnity of the funeral service. Please remember that a calm voice speaking with emotion can convey just as much meaning as hysteria and melodrama. Children need to be reassured, not frightened out of their wits.

🍃 *It's comforting for the mourning children when you direct some of your remarks specifically toward them.*

It is especially soothing for them to hear statements such as "I know how proud your mother/father always was of you/your accomplishments." This applies whether the children are youngsters, teenagers, or grown adults.

🍃 *Be especially considerate to families who have lost a child.*

In the natural course of life, children are supposed to bury their parents and not the other way around. That is why the death of someone's child, whether a baby, teenager, or adult, is considered the greatest loss of all. Speakers giving eulogies need to be extremely careful not to cause the parents any more grief than they're already suffering.

🍃 *Be careful how you address the newly widowed mourner and his/her children.*

Call everyone by their first name or as Ms., Mrs., or Mr. only. Don't use the words *widow* or *orphan* in your eulogy. This creates more emotional pain in the grieving family members.

🍃 *Convey to the bereaved that they have family and friends who care about them.*

It is a tremendously frightening time when someone has lost a loved one. The future seems so dismal and bleak because everyone's lives will now completely change with this death. The bereaved need to be reassured that they will have the continued support and love of their family and friends.

🍃 *Never give the grieving family reason to believe that the deceased won't be a part of their life anymore.*

The deceased most certainly will be thought of and spoken about at all the happy occasions and holidays the family celebrates together, and at the sad times, too. In your eulogy you should "plant" the deceased in the minds of the mourners, not "bury" him!

AFTER THE FUNERAL

Before going to a house of mourning, find out the best time for the family to receive guests. If your emotional state would upset the family members, visit them another time. It is the obligation of close friends and family to keep the atmosphere as calm and peaceful as possible.

Conversation

Take your cues from the bereaved and let them lead the conversation in the direction they want it to go. Do not force them to speak about the deceased. If there is a void in the conversation, do not fill it with empty chatter but let the bereaved reflect on their loss.

The Bereaved's Appetite

People in the beginning stages of grieving often don't have a very strong appetite. Have their favorite foods available for when they are hungry but don't nag them to eat. It is important that they are well hydrated, so have an ample supply of the drinks they like and gently encourage them to drink.

NOTE: Make sure family members on medications have their prescriptions refilled and are taking the correct dosage.

Let the Bereaved Express Their Grief Their Way

Be prepared for dramatic changes in the bereaved's personality, such as continually crying, being very quiet, or unusually talkative. He needs to be able to express his emotions openly and feel comfortable in his own home at this most grievous time.

The Deceased's Belongings

Many widows find it very therapeutic to go through their deceased husband's personal belongings, while others cannot bear the thought of doing this. Let the widow and her children decide when this should be done.

Reminders of the Deceased

There may be pictures/items that are a direct reminder of the deceased that the family does not want to part with and wants prominently displayed. Do not suggest that they be removed because it can be a tremendous comfort to the bereaved to see those pictures/items.

What to Say/What Not to Say

ℐt is often hard to find the right words to say to a person who has suffered a loss, but it can be done. By offering him your heartfelt consolatory words or recounting a heartwarming story about the deceased, you can change the bereaved's whole outlook that day.

The following is a list of phrases intended to guide you on how to interact with someone who has lost a beloved spouse. (Many of the phrases can also be used for a person who lost a child, parent, sibling, or someone else she was extremely close with.)

❧ *"I was very sorry to hear about your loss."*

No other words are necessary because this one sentence conveys your personal sadness.

❧ *"Even though I didn't know your wife/husband, I heard such wonderful things about her/him from other people."*

This is sure to bring a grateful smile to a widow's lips, especially if you can also impart some stories you've heard about the deceased.

🌸 *"I hope it's some comfort for you to know how highly she/he was regarded by all who knew her/him."*

Knowing that the person died with such a sterling reputation is a great solace to the family.

🌸 *"You lost your wife/husband and we lost a close friend. The losses can't be compared, but we also miss her/him very much."*

This statement bonds the friends together in their grief and makes the widow/er not feel so alone in her grief.

🌸 *"What I remember most about her/him was . . ."*

Widow/ers enjoy hearing your special recollections.

* *"Do not think for one moment that anyone at the (wedding, graduation, anniversary party, etc.) will forget who won't be here with us."*

Knowing that your thoughts are on the same wavelength gives the widow a tremendous sense of strength and comfort when she attends the event. (If possible, this should be said before the event and not at the actual affair.)

* *"I can already see that your children are turning out to be such nice young women/men, like their mother/father."*

Comparing their children to a beloved deceased parent is the ultimate praise for the spouse and the children.

🌸 *"It's so nice to see you!"*

Use that phrase for a greeting instead of asking the loaded question, "So, how are you doing?"

🌸 *"I am here for you anytime, day or night, to share the good times and the bad."*

With her emotions going through such an upheaval, it is such a comfort for the widow to know that she has someone to open up to when she is in an upbeat or a melancholy mood.

🌸 *"It's hard to express my sorrow for your loss in person, so I am sending you this card instead."*

It is perfectly acceptable to send a condolence card instead of going over in person or calling them on the phone.

WHAT NOT TO SAY

For a person grieving for her loved one, words play a very important role in how she is able to handle her day-to-day life. Do not upset her by using any of the following phrases:

● *"Oh my goodness, you look terrible!"*

After pulling himself together and trying to face the world after his recent loss, don't pull down the widower by saying that, even if he really does look terrible!

● *"I know how hard your loss must be for you and your children. My kids' pet died a while back and they took it very hard."*

A pet can be considered an integral part of a family, but comparing the loss of an animal to the loss of a human being is unconscionable.

• *"Just be grateful that you were happily married for so many years."*

A person grieving for his spouse is not in any way negating the wonderful years they spent together.

• *"What are you doing with all of your free time, now that you don't have to go to a doctor's office or hospital?"*

A person who now shoulders all of her personal and/or parental responsibilities by herself has no concept of "free time."

• *"My husband/wife travels all the time, so I know how you must feel being alone."*

There is absolutely no correlation between separation by distance and separation by death.

"Let me tell you about the rough time a friend of mine had after she lost her spouse, and how she overcame it."

Uplifting stories are appropriate (at certain times), but horror stories are never appreciated.

"You already married off one child as a widower, so this second time around will be a breeze!"

A widow always feels heartache from her spouse not being at her side at special occasions and needs to be allowed to be sentimental at these times.

"A good night's sleep will do you a world of good."

The widower would love to get a good night's sleep, but he can't because he misses his loving spouse by his side in bed, and he tosses and turns all night because he has so many more responsibilities to focus on now.

"It has been a few months since your spouse died, so just pull yourself together and get on with your life."

The majority of widowers *are* getting on with their lives while dealing with their grief, though it may be a slower process than you are comfortable with.

"Try not to think about your loss."

The intense longing for a loved one gradually diminishes over time, but it is a normal and necessary part of the grieving process.

Memory Gifts

There are many gifts you can give to someone who has suffered a loss, but none as precious as the gift of a memory. As we slowly adjust to life without our loved one, our only link to him is the cherished memories we have. That is why we're delighted when friends and family members give us something tangible that helps keep that person's spirit alive for us. People should never hesitate to make a phone call or send a memento, even if years have passed. For anyone who has lost someone extremely dear to him, dead does not and never will mean forgotten.

GIFT IDEAS

Here are some ways to keep the memories of the deceased alive.

A Birthday Party

Many families make the deceased's birthday a day of celebration instead of a day of sadness. They use the day to celebrate that person's life with a get-together to talk about her/him and share stories. It's a great excuse to order pizza and ice cream for dinner, bring out family albums, and talk to the children and teenagers about their mother or father.

Shared Stories

An individual person can record stories, or a group of family and close friends can get together to reminisce about the deceased. Whether listening to the stories on a CD or watching the person on a DVD, this is truly something the whole family will enjoy. This is especially poignant if you live far away and have never-before-heard stories you would like to share.

The Deceased's Favorite Meal or Treat

If you're making a dish the deceased (and his family) particularly enjoyed eating, make a double recipe and bring it over to his family. The aroma of his favorite dish will elicit wonderful memories.

The Deceased's Favorite Music/Movie

Send along a card to let the family know what it was about the music/movie that the deceased enjoyed so much. If you were with the deceased the first time he heard the music or saw the movie, let the family know what his reaction was and why the music/movie was so meaningful to him.

Souvenirs of Shared Trips

Many friends go on vacations/trips together as single persons or couples. If there are any special pictures or a small memento (e.g., a postcard, seashells, a menu from a restaurant) from those excursions, share them with the deceased's family members.

Letters from People the Deceased Served with in the Armed Services

Enlisted men/women who have served together in life-and-death situations have a special connection. The stories they share of the deceased will be particularly moving to family members.

A Web Page About the Deceased

Since the vast majority of people today are computer literate, it's an easy way for them to find out how the deceased's family is doing and communicate often via e-mail. It's also a wonderful way for people who live far away to share stories and stay connected to the family.

Anything Original the Deceased Created

You may come across a poem the deceased wrote, or a picture she painted, or a song she composed that her family has never seen or heard. These special mementoes are precious to family members who might not have known they existed.

NOTE: It's not necessary to give the family the original copy if it would be hard for you to part with it.

A Letter About the Deceased

This can come from many sources—an employer, teacher, old friend, or someone who knew the deceased very well or even just casually. Definitely write a note to the family if the deceased was a mentor or personal inspiration to you in any way. These letters mean the world to the bereaved because they're a written legacy of how the deceased's life touched others. They are especially important for children who lost their parent at an early age and did not have a chance to get to know her.

Photographs

Families often like to receive photographs of their deceased relative so they can remember him in happier times. These photos could be taken at work, at a neighborhood or community event, at a country club, at a sporting event, at a religious service, or even at their wedding. The pictures don't have to be recent and could also include the following:

- Pictures of him when he was young, playing with a G.I. Joe or bouncing on a trampoline.

- If you attended camp with him, try to find pictures of him involved in a fun camp activity like boating, hiking, swimming, etc.

If he was involved in any sports activity, send a picture of him in his uniform. If the team won any awards, be sure to send a picture of that.

Photos of him if he was an integral part of any student activity in high school or college such as the band, student newspaper, or drama club.

Any graduation pictures from kindergarten on up would be appreciated by loved ones.

Various Memories

There are many concrete ways to preserve memories of the deceased. If you're undertaking a big project, you might want to consult with the relatives of the deceased to see if they'd like to be included in the process. It could be very therapeutic for them to work on something that commemorated their loved one. A few examples of what you can do:

A BOOKLET ABOUT THE FUNERAL SERVICE

This could include the obituaries in the newspapers where the funeral was posted; the program given out at the funeral service and the sign-in register; a copy of the eulogies; the condolence cards sent to the family; a list of who sent over meals; cards from flowers and food baskets sent to the family's home; letters written to family members about the deceased; and a picture of the engraved headstone where the deceased was interred.

A MEMORY BOOK

The memory book can include pictures, poems, or letters written about the deceased, or any other kind of memento the family would appreciate. It doesn't have to be of a serious nature—share funny memories, too. This is an especially meaningful project for classmates to do for a family mourning the loss of a child.

A SCRAPBOOK

Scrapbooking can be a unique, interesting, and fun way to pull together birthday, anniversary, and graduation parties; special events, awards received, trips taken, the births of children and grandchildren, and so on. Be creative and include such things as labels from the deceased's favorite foods, a comic strip he particularly enjoyed, or tickets from a concert, ballgame, or auction you attended with him.

A QUILT

There are many different items associated with the person that you can include in the quilt, such as a piece of clothing from his professional uniform, a scarf or handkerchief, and a letter from his sports jersey. Also, you can iron pictures of the deceased on the quilt. The bereaved will love having a memory quilt she can wrap around her body to completely surround herself with memories of her loved one.

A COLLAGE

The photos can present a time line from her childhood through her adult years, or special, momentous occasions, or holiday pictures and family celebrations, or moments with her children/grandchildren, pictures of good times she had with her spouse and/or close friends, or all of the above! The pictures should be arranged in a logical way, such as chronologically or thematically. Be sure to include a label of when and where each pictures was taken.

Helping Monetarily

he majority of people do not want to accept charity—
they would much rather be on the giving end. Yet some
life situations can force them into dire financial straits, and having
the main breadwinner in the family die is one of them. It is critical to
help them get back on their feet again financially.

Keep in mind the following points:

🌿 Do not make any judgment calls about a family's financial situation. Give them the benefit of the doubt if they say they're experiencing financial difficulties. A good chunk of their money may have been spent on medical expenses. Speak to a close family member or friend and find out what her monetary needs are.

🌿 Do not rely on their rich relatives to foot their bills. The relatives may be helping a great deal or not at all. The point is that you are doing your part to help.

🌿 The family's dignity needs to be preserved. If you are privy to personal financial issues, please keep them confidential. Donations should also be given in a discreet way.

NOTE: If the deceased spouse paid the bills, the surviving spouse may need help organizing a system to pay the bills and keep track of her checkbook balance.

The following are different ways to monetarily help out a family that has suffered a loss.

MAKE SURE THE BREADWINNER
HAS A GOOD, STABLE JOB

The surviving parent certainly will not want to make any immediate changes, but be on the lookout for a job with a higher salary and with better benefits. This may involve paying for her to be retrained or to take classes to get another degree. Also, be sure to alert the family's teenagers of any job opportunities.

A FUND FOR THE CHILDREN

Setting up a fund for the children is one of the most wonderful things you can do. The fund should cover the children's basic needs, and any additional money collected can be put into a college fund, or in CDs or a trust fund. Everything needs to be legally documented, and the people on the committee should have stellar reputations. No one person should have access to the monies collected.

FUNERAL COSTS

Funerals cost thousands of dollars and can be a tremendous financial burden. Contributing to this bill can be enormously helpful.

MEDICAL BILLS

Major medical expenses may have been incurred before
the person died. Find out how much is owed, and see if
you can raise money to eliminate this debt completely.

SCHOOL TUITIONS

The children may be enrolled in private schools/colleges because of the superior quality of the education, or they need to be in an educational institution with peers of their religious background, or the school serves the needs of a child/teenager with disabilities. An education fund that allows them to remain in the school environment they are familiar and comfortable with is crucial. If possible, also raise funds to provide for the children's transportation to and from school.

OUTSTANDING BILLS

It is extremely helpful to the surviving spouse to start off with a clean financial slate. Friends and family members should try to help him pay off his house mortgage, car payments, or credit card bills. Even making a large dent in one of these areas would be a tremendous help.

CLEANING HELP

After a loss, if the home is in complete disarray, it will have a negative effect on the rest of the family. This is one service the family should receive for a year after the death of their loved one.

INDIVIDUAL NEEDS

Many times, the best way to help is to buy something you know the family definitely needs: food, clothing, school uniforms, a computer, school supplies, lawn mower . . . the list is endless! If you own a business that has an item you can offer the family, sell it to them at a reduced rate or give it to them for free. Also, you can offer them a cheaper version of last year's inventory *only* if you are sure they will not be insulted. Present your offer to them in the least embarrassing way possible. A wonderful way to do this is to contribute privately: buy them store gift certificates and send them anonymously.

Special Gifts for the Bereaved

*T*hough sending a gift to someone who has suffered a loss won't take away all her emotional pain, trying to add some joy to her life will absolutely make her feel better. To show your support, buy specific gifts you know the person will particularly enjoy.

The gifts listed in this section can also be given to a person who is ill, or to their main caregiver, or to a close family member. This applies to children and teenagers as well.

THINGS TO CONSIDER

When to Give a Gift

Anytime the mood strikes you is a good time to send a present that is sealed with your love. If you are close to the person, you'll know when she needs a bit of a lift. If you're not so close, it can be a spur-of-the-moment decision. It may be the furthest thing from your mind, and then you'll chance upon the perfect card, or gift, or an idea for a gift, and right there and then your decision to get it for your friend will be made.

It's always a good time to send a present around a special anniversary, birthday, holiday, or a date that holds a special significance for that person. At these times she'll need your love and support the most. You don't have to send an elaborate present; a card or flowers will do.

Gift certificates should have an expiration date of at least a year, so the bereaved can use them when the time is right for him. Don't constantly ask him if he has used your present; he doesn't need that added pressure on top of everything else. Let him use it when he is in the mood to enjoy it.

How Much to Spend

When buying a gift for a friend or family member, don't exceed your means. Many gift items are available at reasonable prices, even if you have to downscale a bit: for example, a smaller bottle of the bereaved's favorite perfume.

If there's something you know the bereaved would really love to have but it's beyond your financial means, maybe you can purchase it with a group of friends. For instance, while one group of friends can afford to send the bereaved for a weekend stay at a bed and breakfast, a group with more substantial means can afford to send her on a cruise. The bereaved will appreciate the gift no matter how lavish or simple it is.

PAMPERING

No matter how much people try to deny it, everyone has an innate need to completely indulge himself now and then in something that he likes.

Yet there are certain times when the need for pampering is greater, and one of them is after a person loses a beloved spouse, child, or parent. The bereaved is dealing with intense grief on a daily basis, and it will do him a world of good to be able to relax for a few hours—or a few days.

The following is a list of pampering gifts.

A Professional Massage

With soft music playing, dimmed lights, and a calming atmosphere, it is a surefire way to totally unwind. If the person can't venture outside her house, arrange for the masseuse to give her a massage in her home.

A Day at a Spa

This is the ultimate TLC treatment gift; completely in-dulging oneself does wonders for the body and spirit! But if for any reason the person feels uncomfortable visiting a spa (she might not have the time), simply treat her to a manicure, pedicure, and facial. She may even prefer to divide up this gift and use it three different times.

A Kit to Relax in the Bath

Buy a wicker basket and fill it with soap, shampoo, condi-
tioner, bubble bath, fluffy sponges, a good book, a new
towel, and, to be really impressive, maybe a new terry-
cloth robe! Your present will be too enticing to resist and
your friend/family member will make the time to
enjoy a long and luxurious bath.

A Gift Certificate to a Favorite Store

Even the closest friend can have trouble finding the perfect gift for someone going through a hard time. At these times, the best thing to give is a gift card. It can be redeemable at an entire mall, at a store your friend likes to shop in, or even at his favorite restaurant. Include a note saying that he should splurge one day when he really needs it—your treat!

A Trip

Offer your friend/family member a trip of his choice (within your budget, of course). Frequent-flyer miles can be used to purchase the tickets. This trip can be given to an individual or can include the whole family. Find out first when the best time is for your friend to travel, so that he'll have time to make arrangements for his job, children, or any social obligations. A change of scenery usually does wonders for someone who is grieving; it helps lift his spirits and can change his whole mind-set.

A Piece of Jewelry

This is especially a good idea if the person has an important occasion/event coming up. A new necklace for a woman or cuff links for a man can brighten their spirits, especially if they are hosting the event. There may have been a regular occasion when the widow received a piece of jewelry from her husband, such as her birthday or their anniversary. It's completely appropriate to give her a gift of jewelry at that time, especially the first time she celebrates it without her beloved spouse.

A Live Performance

This can range from a local community theater production to a Broadway play. The person may enjoy attending the play accompanied just by you, or having a group of friends go with him. To give your gift a little more pizzazz, include lunch or dinner before or after the performance.

THINKING OUTSIDE THE BOX

In the weeks and months following a funeral, it is so nice to receive presents that show you have truly put some thought into them. Bring your friend a present he'll actually enjoy receiving by focusing on what he likes to read, do, and listen to; or buy or make something new that you think he'd appreciate. Make sure that the present can be exchanged easily if he would prefer something else. Here are some examples:

Entertainment

A set of his favorite movies or TV shows makes a great gift. People who have suffered a loss need some downtime. One of the best ways you can help them do this is with DVDs of movies or TV shows they enjoy—his favorite shows help him escape his demanding pressures for a little while. To make your gift a little more special, find out your friend's favorite movie snack. Then buy him a huge bowl with his name on it and fill it with his favorite treat.

For the Car

Many people spend hours in their cars each week, traveling back and forth to work, doing children's carpools, or running errands. This may be the only time of the day when they're free from household/work pressures. You can buy them audiobooks, a new CD of their favorite singer or group; a hanging air freshener to make their car smell good; a box filled with their favorite treats; or a new thermos for their morning coffee fix. These gifts can be given individually or as a boxed present. Another nice gesture is to buy an updated version of a emergency road kit—and show them how to use it.

Home Décor

Many people appreciate getting a gift that lends their home a new and different look and gives the family members a bit of a boost after their loved one has died. A flowering plant in a ceramic pot, a colorful tablecloth with matching napkins, a set of towels with a color-coordinated bathroom mat and shower curtain for the bathroom, or even new handles for the kitchen cabinets.

A Personalized Gift

People especially enjoy presents with pictures of their family, friends, or pets. If you're planning to give this type of present make it one that is useful to your friend, such as an office coffee mug with her dog's picture, a kitchen calendar with photos of her children/grandchildren, or a picture frame for her den engraved with "To the Big Boss, From Your Loyal Employees"—and include a picture of everyone hard at work.

Homemade Presents

The time and effort you put into making these gifts will really mean a lot to your friend. A wooden bird feeder, an embroidered jewelry box, a chime to hang outside the front door, a trivet for the kitchen counter, a painted picture, decorative throw pillows, a shawl or scarf, or beaded jewelry.

A Personal Journal

It can be a good emotional release for many people to write down their thoughts and feelings and see them clearly expressed in their own handwriting. Reading over their notes can be very therapeutic as they see the small and large steps they've made in their grieving process. And this portable gift can easily be slipped into a purse or briefcase.

Any Product with a Scent

The study of aromatherapy has shown that aromas can lift our spirits, relax us, and help induce sleep. Buy your friend different kinds of scented candles, scented pillows, new kinds of spices for baking, or a new kind of perfume or cologne. She may like a scented gift for her office, too.

Craft

Find out what your friend's favorite hobby is. She might enjoy receiving a new needlepoint kit complete with the yarn or embroidery threads she will need, new gardening tools and seeds to start her spring garden, a cookbook and covered casserole dish to try out scrumptious new recipes, or a new specialized tool for her home workshop. She may not have felt like starting any new projects since she suffered her loss, and this gift may give her the incentive to do so.

Gift Subscriptions

Many people enjoy reading fashion, business, computer, sports, or specific men's/women's magazines, so buy your friend/family member a subscription to a new one that he doesn't have. Or buy him tickets to regional theater shows in his community, season passes for baseball games, or even annual passes to a local museum or zoo. If you can't afford to treat him to a season pass, buying him a ticket to one game is also fine.

Special Activities to Do with the Bereaved

A friend who has suffered a loss may be hesitant to step out into the world and resume his daily life. Offering to do activities with him is one of the best ways to help him ease back into society. It is much easier for him to face people when he has a friend by his side.

ON A BEAUTIFUL DAY

- Ride bicycles in the countryside.

- Have a picnic in the park.

- Take a slow stroll in your neighborhood or an invigorating walk on a nature trail.

- Have a backyard barbecue adult style—steaks, not hot dogs!

- Strap on binoculars and go bird watching.

- Walk on a beach or a boardwalk.

- Enjoy an espresso at an outdoor café.

ON A BEAUTIFUL NIGHT

- Go for a car ride along a lit scenic route.

- Set up lawn chairs and watch what's going on around the neighborhood.

- Have drinks on the patio.

- Drive to a secluded spot outside the town limits and enjoy the peace and quiet.

- Borrow a telescope and gaze at the stars.

- Eat dinner at an outdoor restaurant.

- Build a campfire and roast marshmallows.

NOTE: Evening hours can be especially hard for someone who has suffered a loss, so doing something with her then is a nice idea.

Regular weekly get-together

Organize a women's/men's night out, to play cards,
pool, board games, or work on a puzzle or a quilt.

Set a time for a friendly game of any sport he is interested in playing

A vigorous sports game is a lot of fun and a great
tension reliever.

- ***Join an exercise class—step, aerobics (regular or aquatic), spinning, or Tae Bo***

  A good idea physically and mentally stimulating, too.

- ***Take a baking course***

  Learning how to make the perfect omelet, discovering new ways to cook delicious low-fat meals, or baking rich, elegant desserts can be quite pleasurable.

🍃 *Join a book club*

Even if you and your friend have very different literary tastes, this is a great way to be exposed to many different kinds of writing styles and authors.

🍃 *Take an academic class*

Find out if your friend would enjoy taking a course that might have more relevance for her now, such as finance—investing wisely for the future or effective home management.

Take a painting, pottery, or calligraphy class

Regardless of artistic ability, it is very relaxing to work with different materials and colors.

Practice yoga

Yoga is so healthy for the mind and body: it gives a person time to relax and breathe a little and get off the emotional rollercoaster he has been on since the death of his loved one.

❧ *Attending a grief counseling class*

Your friend may need your physical support to attend a grief counseling class, or to meet privately with a grief counselor, or to help him find a safe chat room on the internet for grieving spouses or to spend time in the library finding appropriate books on grief.

❧ *Get involved in a new activity*

Find an activity that is new and different: learning to ride a horse, playing an instrument, practicing karate, joining a choir, learning photography, or trying out for a role in a local community theater.

Volunteer at a nonprofit organization

Once a loved one dies, family members have a great need to be on the giving end instead of the receiving end, so help them find places that need volunteers like soup kitchens, senior citizen centers, local hospitals, nursing homes, adult literacy programs, and local schools.

Garden

Buy flower bulbs or vegetable seeds and plant them with your friend: after someone dies, it is healing to see things blossom and grow.

🍂 *Engage in warm/cold-weather activities*

For people who enjoy the warm weather, take them out for a day of swimming, surfing, scuba diving, or fishing. If you own a boat invite the bereaved out for the day or weekend, or book a day trip on a boat. For those who prefer cold weather activities, suggest ice skating, sledding, or skiing. If possible, take them to a ski lodge for a few days.

🍂 *Take a tour*

Find out if there are any interesting day tours that the bereaved would be interested in going on, from traveling out of town on a bus/train or just a walking tour in his own city.

Through the Years

ime is a great healer, yet those who have suffered a crushing loss want to remain closely connected to their family and friends and, at times, still need to be showered by their love and attention.

KEEPING IN CONTACT

As soon as you get home from the funeral, mark a date on the calendar to contact your friend.

Phone calls and visitors diminish as the weeks pass, so if you are a casual acquaintance, call her a few weeks later and see how she is doing, invite her out to lunch/dinner, or drop off a small gift or a home-baked treat. If you are a close friend you will probably be in daily contact with her, so take your cue from her actions and tone of voice and know when to be there for her and when to let her grieve privately.

REMEMBER DATES THAT
HOLD SPECIAL SIGNIFICANCE

Widows feel a tremendous emotional build-up before birthdays, anniversaries, or the date the spouse died, so be sure to call her on that day. Also, call a few days before to see if she wants company or if there is something specific she would like you to do with her, like visiting the cemetery.

INCLUDE THE BEREAVED
IN YOUR CELEBRATIONS

Your bereaved friend will still want to be invited to your celebrations. Send him an invitation, but don't pressure him to attend if he's not ready to socialize in public.

HELP THE BEREAVED
WITH THEIR CELEBRATIONS

Call and ask what you can do before or after the event.
There are innumerable tasks and errands that you can
help out with—just ask!

BUY RANDOM CARDS TO SEND

The cards can be inspirational, funny, religious, or commending your friend on how he is handling life's challenges. It is important for him to know he has your support as he strives to heal emotionally.

CHILDREN'S EVENTS

Offer to go with a single parent to an event that her child is in, such as a tennis match, a musical performance, or a graduation ceremony. It is important that she has someone by her side to share her happiness with.

HOLIDAYS

In general, holidays are a particularly difficult time for a widower. Be sure to include him and his family in your holiday plans.

IF THERE IS A PARTICULAR EVENT THE WIDOW ATTENDED WITH HER HUSBAND, ASK IF YOU CAN ACCOMPANY HER

She may still want to attend but it might be too hard for her to go by herself. Offer to go with her even if you have no interest in fashion shows, operas, or sporting events. By accompanying your friend and making her happy, you will enjoy your evening out, too!

What I Should Say

What I Should Not Say

GIFTS TO BRING TO THE ILL PERSON AT THE HOSPITAL

GIFTS TO BRING TO THE ILL PERSON AT HOME

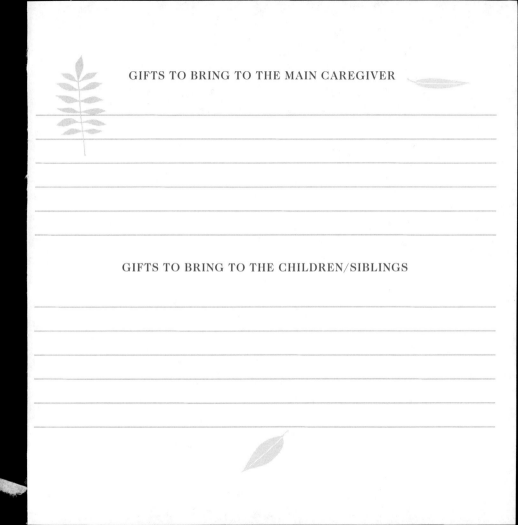

GIFTS TO BRING TO THE MAIN CAREGIVER

GIFTS TO BRING TO THE CHILDREN/SIBLINGS

Significant Dates to Remember

NAME	DATE	OCCASION